The Brink

Jacob Polley was born in Carlisle in 1975.
In 2002 he won the Arts Council of England/
BBC Radio 4 'First Verse' Award and also received
a major Eric Gregory Award in the same year.
The Brink is his first collection of poems.

The Brink
Jacob Polley

PICADOR

First published 2003 by Picador
an imprint of Pan Macmillan Ltd
Pan Macmillan, 20 New Wharf Road, London N1 9RR
Basingstoke and Oxford
Associated companies throughout the world
www.panmacmillan.com

ISBN 0 330 41288 4

1 3 5 7 9 8 6 4 2

A CIP catalogue record for this book is available from
the British Library.

Typeset by SX Composing DTP, Rayleigh, Essex
Printed and bound in Great Britain by
Mackays of Chatham plc, Chatham, Kent.

for Caleb and Miriam

Contents

A Jar of Honey, 3

Declaration, 4

Economics, 6

Room, 7

Moving House, 8

Smoke, 10

The Crow, 13

Salvage, 14

Drover, 16

The North–South Divide, 17

The Boast, 19

Salmonary, 21

from Definitions for the Wife, 23

Man, 24

The Snag, 25

Allhallows, 27

First Light, 28

Saturday Matinee, 29

The Gulls, 30

Snow, 31

Fish, 32

Friday, 34

The Grey Goose, 35

The Irish Sea, 36

Attic, 37

The Distance, 39

The Remedy, 40

Crabbing, 41

The Kingdom of Sediment, 42

Acknowledgements

Acknowledgements are due to the editors of *First Pressings* (Faber & Faber), *Franks Casket*, *Pitch*, the *Cumberland News* and *News and Star*, where versions of some of these poems first appeared.

'The Boast' was published in the catalogue that accompanied Donald Wilkinson's exhibition of paintings, *A Wider Landscape* (The Wordsworth Trust, 2002).

'The Distance' first appeared in *Earth Has Not Anything to Show More Fair* (The Wordsworth Trust/Shakespeare's Globe, 2002).

'Moving House' and 'Salmonary' were first broadcast on BBC Radio 4, and 'Room' was commissioned and broadcast by BBC Radio 4 on National Poetry Day, 2002.

A number of these poems first appeared in a pamphlet published by Northern Lights in 2001.

The author is grateful to Cumbria County Council, Northern Arts, New Writing North, The Society of Authors, the Arts Council of England and Dr Robert Woof and all at the Wordsworth Trust for their help and support.

The Brink

A Jar of Honey

You hold it like a lit bulb,
a pound of light,
and swivel the stunned glow
around the fat glass sides:

it's the sun, all flesh and no bones
but for the floating knuckle
of honeycomb
attesting to the nature of the struggle.

Declaration

Certainly there were squabbles –
such-and-such's dog let loose
and scrabbling among so-and-so's flower beds,
the bellyache of those few stolen apples,
but the cows came home and calved in the sheds,
and the night may have cleared its throat
below the window but was soon on its way,
the locks held and the barges stayed afloat,
the moon made the most of the empty rails;

shadows were the only things thrown
to the ground at the opening of back doors,
curtains met when they were drawn
and the thought of our tea lay,
undisturbed in the reservoir till morning,
electricity did good around the house,
the coal shrugged, the fire settled back in the grate;
there were measurements, but they were inaccurate

and happily so, books kept at room temperature
or a little below, and if there were broken plates
it was one at a time, and doctors cured
what they could or gave it to us, short and straight;
queues formed, bread was baked
and the embarrassment of a bad note
wouldn't silence an orchestra;
decisions were taken, clocks wound, roads swept,

orders were given lightly, from far away
and the papers said what they had to say,
work continued, letters were written,
neighbours hung the shapes of themselves out to dry
and if attempts were made to change the skin
they were cosmetic and reasonable;
the sea dragged on, fog rolled in,
guards blew into their fists

and as borders were closed and streets were blocked
our black kettles sang on our blue gas hobs
and if names were listed and names ticked off
there was no cause for alarm, no hiding in lofts;
couples strolled, waiters snapped white tablecloths
and neither cries for help nor the pistol shots
lifted the starlings from our rooftops.

Economics

My father at the sink
like his father before him
softening two flints
of soap, then squeezing
the yellow into the pink.

Room

For another bone in the stock,
cup of water in the soup,
more of the plate,
more fresh air in the baking of the cake;

for more bread
through the butter, more knee
through the trouser leg;

for a longer washing line,
wider photograph,
extra drawers;

for another face
but it's full of yours.

Moving House

Bubble-wrap the chimney like a vase,
its bouquet of wilted smoke
tipped out, and pack the slates
the way you'd box a brittle set of books.
You'll find the attic can't be moved
once the sky floods in, though another will appear
when the last trickle's wrung from the new roof
and the dark takes place between the rafters.

Flat-pack each room, careful not to tear
the windows away from their views:
they must be eased on to their fresh prospects
to keep their perspectives true;
lead the bath out by the plug chain,
its tin legs squealing, and poke the electricity
from its hole with a forked stick,
pinning it to the ground by the throat.

Carry the doors on your backs,
for they've leant so heavily against the world
they deserve this one good turn;
the foundations will make their own way –
tap the ground gently when you arrive
and they'll rise to the surface like worms
after rain.
            Should you not have time to memorise
these instructions, to squeeze all the air

out of the stairs;
should you be so utterly unprepared
as to leave your house behind,
rooms thrown around their walls
by the bare bulbs swinging in your wake;
should you have nowhere to set those thoughts,
fumbled at the beginning of the day
and caught again in a sunlit doorway,

nowhere for the table and chairs to stretch
their old shadows every afternoon
or the floorboards to query each footstep –
bury them, deep in the woods,
and fashion new ones by the glow
of your little camp fire, as wolves howl
high in the snow-covered hills
and the stars whistle over your head.

Smoke

My father kept a stove
with dog's legs
on a pink hearthstone.

One morning he climbed down the icy stairs
and spread his palms
on the blood-warm metal flanks.

He cranked open the iron doors,
like a black bank safe's,
but found no heat and ash heaped in its place.

He cracked grey whittled coals,
released brief blue flames,
and knocked downy soot through the bars of the grate.

The ash-pan, softly loaded
and almost as wide as a doorway,
he carried like dynamite through the dark house,

his bright face blown with smuts.
At the back door
he slid the ash into a tin dustbin,

then snapped sticks,
crumpled newspaper,
struck a match

and dipped it between the kindling.
Smoke unrolled, flames spread,
the rush of the stove eating air started up,

and my father would shake on rocks
from an old coal hod
and swing the doors shut.

But this time
he took a book, broke its spine
and slung that on instead:

his diaries,
year by year,
purred as their pages burned,

their leather boards shifted, popped
and fell apart.
Soon I would arrive,

pulled from under my mother's heart,
and grow to watch my father
break the charred crossbeam of a bird from the flue,

wondering if I too
had hung in darkness and smoke,
looking up at the light let down her throat
whenever my mother sang or spoke.

The Crow

Once Cain had done for Abel
he peeled off his gloves,
rolled them up tight
and set them alight.
It was then they were blackened into life,
already at the wind's throat.

Salvage

The shadows in this house are black sails,
stuffed with spiders now the wind won't fill them
and they hang from joists of crossed ship's spars
that still hold a hull's curve
and notches where the ribs of a keel were fixed.

Maybe there's a mast among them
but it's pegged to the rest to frame the room
where you lie, listening to the rafters creak.

Because all wood cut locally has a weak twist
spun into it by the storms that tear up the estuary
and through their leafless forests,
men must have parted the timbers of a beached boat
with the same relish they'd bone a fish:

whoever claimed a wreck would have a house,
built like Adam out of clay
and braced on crook-beams, rough with salt.

The only risk was waking in darkness,
convinced a draught was the breath of a castaway
who'd staggered this far,
flopped onto his stomach and had a roof raised
out of his rattling shoulder blades,

his skeleton cured and reclad with clay
and his limbs chopped into the bricks
used to build the walls that gather the garden
to the house, as if to warm it into flower
with its false heart of fire and nests of mice.

Drover

Father of my father's father,
greasy breeches, bow legs – keeper
of that habitual early hour
when the cattle hardly move for fear
of trotting off the precipice
hidden by the morning mist.

I want to say, *Little father,*
leave the fields, forget the fodder,
the nag's dead, long live the Ford –
you'll be buried in an oat-sack, lined with straw.

He hawked and spat and carried on
carting hay to the stables of London,
scorning the combustion engine
and those 'wet wethers', bleating
before their progressive forces:
'men will always get ahead on horses.'

The North–South Divide

fills with flood-water;
the bows of Scotland lift clear
of the Atlantic, cod roam
the East Anglian plains, kelp
throttles Sherwood, the chimneys
of the Midlands slowly barnacle,
Cumbria tilts;
congers lie in catacombs
cold-wiring our relics,
our kings' bones;
a whale hangs a moment
singing in the vault
of St Paul's, men dive
through their Southern libraries,
where crabs unpick the calfskin
of our histories;
Stratford-under-Avon
is swanless and rip-tidal,
hagfish haunt Leicester Square,
anglerfish twinkle
through Trafalgar's oyster beds.
Look from Manchester
out to sea: the South you knew
from quiz shows and road maps,
from nursery rhymes and bad news
is gathering a storm

to its heaving,
gull-broached,
heavy-breakered bosom.

The Boast

There's nothing soft about our snow:
it collapses like a ceiling
out of the sky, crushes our cars,
blasts all the tree trunks white
up the same side, while sheep shiver,
dreadlocked with frost.

It comes mountain-sized,
accommodating fells
so they can dress up as glaciers
and dream of throwing their weight
down new, deserted centuries.

It covers milestones, signposts and crossroads,
buries the bus stops
where our elderly climb down
with their pebble-filled rucksacks
and sticks to test the surface;
builds them into its blizzard walls –

the toy-bright colours
of their stiffened anoraks
blooming secretly in blocks of ice –
until the thaw, when they're broken
between stones.
                        Life, death?

A snowfield separates them –
the foot and a half fallen on the graveyard
so all but the angels
on tiptoes, with trumpets to breathe through,
are tucked away; the church bells throttled,
the hymnbooks frozen to the pews.

You could walk it:
the pines, like flour merchants,
clapping their powdery hands,
a crow, spilling its wings
from its own inkstand
and trickling into the distance;
your breath thrown over your shoulder.

Beyond the crisply folded hills
it's said another season brings our neighbours' fields
   around,
that their becks and brooks and streams
glitter and twist, like silver threads,
as the sun pulls them up through the ground.

Salmonary

for Susan Tranter

This, first edition of fish,
fillets recto/verso,
a zincky blue portfolio
with an eye, ringed in gold leaf,

turned to the kitchen ceiling.
Slipcase, soft back, uncracked spine –
imagine it cruising
midstream, set against the close grain

of the river's current,
intractable as shadow.
Or think of the failure of seas
to swing this jaw

back on its ruminative hinge.
Somehow oceans wound up
in this skull's square inch:
five epics in a nutshell.

Inscriptions on a fish scale.
Yet, when it goes under the grill,
tuned to the softest gas flame,
it's our mouths that fill

with a fathom of water.
This gauntlet
of gently rusted armour
I lay between us:

it's for us to chew over,
to take issue,
not with each other
but with the arrangement

of sea salt and coarse pepper
on the tongue,
with the backbone
and finer points of fish grammar.

Already the butter's
loose in the margins,
illuminating
the edge of each plate;

so here's the fish knife,
here's the fork,
find your place
marked with parsley

and begin.

from Definitions for the Wife

Commiseration:
waiting outside the chip shop
with his fishing rod.

Man

Take up the carpets and apply weather
to the front door until it begrudges its frame.
Chip the gloss work, riddle the earth with stones –
let the tap spit out its washer.

Flaunt greasy ceilings and empty walls,
loosen floorboards and the bog seat,
block the sink, break the circuit,
have him make a necessity of six-inch nails.

Grieve him to look deeply into the machine
and chronicle its black decline
in a rag with an already spotted history –
thistle the lawn, rot the tree.

Hail whitewash, the improvement of echoes
by tiling, the burial of the dog,
the sundry Sundays of God-foreseen odd jobs
when your man might less than idly suppose

that he could drag open the great toolbox,
descend its short flight of steps
and have them fold away over his head.

The Snag

The moon's too full
the tide won't turn
and the breakers pile up unbroken
far along the silent coast.

Back out of the black sky
smoke trundles
and the hearth fire finds its shadows
too heavy to cast against the parlour walls.

The night air's dropped everything
to pick up your scent:
in still fields, cattle shoulder
ropes of breath,

and the drunk's left
to carry his own voice
below the bedrooms where sleep walks
with no appetite, among the open-eyed.

What's my point? It falls short
like the sighting of dead stars
by their twinkle
in all those naked eyes,

my love, my rhythm, my rest:
as if I could snag this night
in these lines, faster than the east
ties the dark off with that pink knot.

Allhallows

Morning breaks like an egg
or a promise, and the gulls
fall about laughing. The skulls
you lugged home
from the farmer's oddest field
are candle-cooked,
as if one black thought
had burnt itself out,
and the sheets are back on the beds,
their eye-sockets sewn up.
The masks lie, knocked off,
so return your warts
to the cereal box
and observe the single brown bite
in the apple still nodding
in the washing-up bowl.
You've held a torch beneath your chin
and your face has stuttered
through your hidden selves
on its cylinder of bone:
now you're wondering which look
you slept on, which you woke with,
or if your face has come to rest
between two looks, on emptiness.

First Light

The new couch, wrapped in plastic,
sits outside the showroom.
The rain drips down the inside
of each green tree, though the sun's
baking the glaze off tiles and paving stones;
and in the old black paint on the back door
the cracks appear, red raw.

Saturday Matinee

Maybe it's raining and all the best shop doorways
are sheltered in, a ruthlessness of umbrellas
has taken to the streets, everybody's
lost to the sound of their own private storm,
and you're thinking about the lobby
with carpets as red as riddled embers,
the consolations of buttered popcorn,
your ticket-half threaded on an usher's string,
the darkness where you find your flip-down seat, sit,
and watch the house lights for the nod and the wink,
then sneak a look at the rows behind
as the curtains skate apart and strangers
catch the brightness of this idea
full in the face, their mouths blown open
and eyes given up, and you too will turn
as the title falls away from the screen,
to follow her through the depth of the gold dust
swirled down the length of the projectionist's beam.

The Gulls

They're trying to shake themselves out of their sleeves
in the air above the bins,
their flight suddenly akin
to dangling on a coat hook
by the back of the coat you're still in.

Snow

It survives in quiet places
like a rare species
whose habitat is silence
and closed roads. It upholsters
the empty park bench
with long creaking bolsters
and lags the fields like draughty lofts.
Look up – the night's in pieces
or the moon's sieving
its desiccated seas;
there's a glamour about the roofs
and even the old car
on bricks in the yard seems natural,
tucked up to the axles
in this delicate impasse.
Bridle path and motorway unite
under the wastes of space
each gale force renovates,
and only the cat and the blackbird
betray themselves so neatly
in the lawn's flawless enamouring
that we'll forgive their few footnotes
at dawn, when we open our doors
and the hard-packed white light
leant against them falls in.

Fish

What do they mean
these mackerel crowds,
the gaunt salmon crashing upstream,
the eels on the fields in the rain,
coupling and uncoupling,
like iron escaped
from a blacksmith's bucket;

the pike, deep in the poem
of its own prehistory,
working fat lips around the off-rhyme
of that jaw; the sturgeon and small fry,
those carried by the Romans,
like new gods, and installed in dark northern tarns
to outlast them and Empire;

the Arctic char
left over by the last ice age
in an English lake,
the shoals of herring,
the air and grace
of the brown trout as it skips
the pages of the weir;

the carp, maintained in hothouses
and snow-gardens,
smouldering ponderously in sunken hearths,
the ballan wrasse and bass;
the cod 'boat-anglers can contact all year round',
leaving the lines dead
and men to brood over the implausible emptiness?

See them out of the corners of your eyes
wrapped in yesterday's parables
or as dorsal fins, shearing up the page
you're reading down,
to spawn and die
at the beginning again.

They endure despite us:
in heavy industry's backwaters
and gravel pits, chub grow monstrous
and the old glory holes of progress,
the pools of coolant, the flooded kilns and chemical moats,
are smelting their own moving parts.

Friday

The book of white magic
pored over in the steamy light
of the supper table, its gist
flaked easily from the bone.

The Grey Goose

The grey goose
of the North Atlantic
shuffles at the base of these cliffs,

never sits too long
on one rock, shipwreck
or lower dock step.

Her great breast settles
over every cove,
puts the white coast on the wane.

Her beak's buried in the crook
of a green wing,
until she's poked

by lightning:
then she plucks men
from their boats.

The Irish Sea

If ever a sea was going nowhere,
rolling back on itself, its handbrake off,
running itself ragged, thrown to wind-dogs;
horizon empty, fishing grounds bare,
a sea of only so many layers.
The moon pulls them away. What have you got?
More old rope, dead wood; beauty's blind spot.
A little sad reflection and you're there,
the end of the line, the long haul hauled
to the brink, the drink, from Paul back to Saul.

Attic

Eject the birds from the tree,
let the milk bottles' white bombshells
be held in crates, in far-off dairies;
gather up the stairs, snap shut the staircase,
leave it standing outside the bedroom door

and lie a little longer barefoot, loose-haired,
unaware. The grocers sleep, the Quakers sit,
as they have for three and a half centuries,
in silence. Whatever manuals, minutes,
manifestos, protocols and directives say –

however much water must be moved
from hills undone by ceaseless rain
to change the kettle's tone, let it stay.
Dust blows through the blinds, the sun breaks in,
the walls reappear. The mirror's lit:

away with it. Forget you had pockets,
a fish-lure of keys or an old *A–Z*
whose squint alleys and abbreviated courts,
its injunctions against going nowhere,
lost you once among brick lanes and wind-chilled squares.

Let the day go to waste in this little room,
the sky darken, the window cool;
let the city arrive at the edge of the afternoon,
where we can look out from bed
at the roofs and the moon.

The Distance

I can feel your heart through the back of the chair:
yes, it's me, standing over your shoulder
as you pass your hand over your hair.

There are cities, ports, into whose harbours
drift whole districts with their ballrooms and kitchens,
places where the earth is cracked open

and men climb down with their own minds
thrown out in front of them.
So what should you care

if I dipped one hand into the current
and changed the course of your black hair,
the better to hold my breath to your throat?

The Remedy

Sprigs of unspoken nettle
nipped from their new green stems
at midnight, the moon engrossed,
the sky blue as a brandy-flame.
Boiled, mashed with oats
and boiled again –
the goose-grey first light firing the curtains
and the lamps beginning to wilt.
Taken upstairs to the sick man,
who's lain so long undiagnosed
his kicked-off leather boots
lie broken like moulds,
and put to his lips: the strength to name
his affliction, spoon by awkward spoon.

Crabbing

for Darja Heikkilä

To the fishmonger's for a cod's head
glistering like pencil lead,
a Stone Age axe.
Down to the harbour's edge
where the water takes deep breaths,
beer bottles scrape the harbour wall
and men spread nets
for the spotless gulls to inspect.
Tie it to a fishing line and lower away,
the sea swinging shut against the granite stairwell
that climbs down into the oily dark.
Wait five minutes, ten,
for as long as you can stand
to watch the tide rise and the tide fall
with the catgut biting your hand,
then draw the fish-head up.
Struggling under the weight of their shells
in the air, the crabs hang –
legs like picklocks, mechanical claws.
Keep them in a bucket on the quay
till the end of the day,
then tip them out, count them
and kick them back into the sea.

The Kingdom of Sediment

I

Rust seemed to bleed downstream
from dumped washing tubs and pram wheels,
the way sheep leaked poison
as they lay dead at the source,
the taste sharp as smashed glass
if you cupped hands and sipped.

Our stream smelled of pennies sweating in a fist
and ran out from behind houses
into farmland. There, we mud-pied cows,
safe on one side as the herd wobbled, shy
at the water's edge, engrossed
in its broken reflection.

Sometimes we found a door
in a field. We'd shunt it into the stream,
then follow with branches, poking it sideways,
hoping it wouldn't wedge between banks:
when it stuck, we'd dare each other to step on,
though I was sure it would swing open

under me, as doors did when I leant against them
listening in, and pitch me through to the kingdom
of sediment, where leeches bled your shins

and bicycle spokes and ragged tins
slit the balls of your feet to the bone.

II

To the sewage works at the edge of town
I was led and drowned
while my brother kicked pebbles at a can,
furious when his shots flew wide and swam
under the slurry, breaking out trapped gas
as they were sucked down.

I was drawn by sticklebacks, through overflow pipes,
picking up the accent of the current
as I babbled down arterial byways:
I found my new tongue
could run around anything.

As the youngest under
I ascended to the throne,
ruling suicides and sea-fishermen
who've stolen into fresh water
to escape the gaping spaces of the ocean.

Sometimes I caress familiar ankles.
I hold them as the feet paddle,
but my hands shatter when they climb back out;
I feel heat beneath the skin,
and long to break the surface.

My sceptre was cast from flakes of iron
and mercury, siphoned from a salmon's gills;
my robes are trimmed with white-water,
my crown inlaid with bubbles, caught
while they still held flawless pearls of breath.

My orb is a kingfisher's egg
that rolled into the water as it hatched.
The fledgling peers from the crack
or lifts half its shell and shows me wings,
sodden at its sides. It knows no grief.
I tell it stories about above.